Advance Praise for
The Resilience

It has been more than se~~~~~~~~~~~~~~~~~~ from the concentration camps ~~~~~~~~~~~~~~ happened can never be forgotten an~~~~~~~~~~ever be changed. But what I have learned over time is that I have the choice on how to respond to the past—I can allow it to define me and direct my every action or I can recognize that bad things happen to everyone. Suffering is universal but victimhood is optional.

My friend Pattie Vargas has learned that victimhood is an inside job and she shares her journey out of that prison in this beautiful book. The things that happen to us don't have to be the final chapter unless we choose to let it be so. Her insights on maintaining an overcomer mindset are necessary to anyone seeking freedom from the past and hope for an empowered future.

—Dr. Edith Eva Eger
Therapist, Speaker, Educator
Author of *The Choice: Embrace the Possible*

If life is what happens while we're busy making plans, Pattie Vargas' new book, *The Resilience Factor is Your Superpower,* is an account of how she woke up and overcame the fear of living to her full potential. It's an illuminating story for all women who strive to balance love, life, and career goals. We are more resilient than we may think and Vargas shows how to tap into it.

—René Street
Executive Director
American Business Women's Association

Pattie Vargas and I have been colleagues and friends since 2004. In that time, I have watched her flex and adapt to changes in her personal and professional life with charm, grace and confidence. I often wondered, "Damn, how does she do it?!" Well, now I know. It's the Resilience Factor that she named, claimed and continues to refine as she travels through life. We can all learn a few critical slices of advice from this wonderful book about not letting circumstances define us and how to craft the next chapter of our own story. Oh yeah, she's a rockstar speaker and thought leader as well!

—Michelle Bergquist
CEO & Co-Founder - Connected Women of Influence
Co-Founder - SUE Talks
Founding Partner - Women Lead Publishing

Does it feel like life continually pummels you? An imaginary cloud always looms overhead? You can't seem to catch a break on the job, in your marriage...in life? As a pastor and counselor for over 20 years, I've heard those words, sometimes phrased differently, but always with a sense of hopelessness and pain! I love the quote by Chuck Swindoll from his book, Grace Awakening. It reads: *"I am convinced that life is 10% what happens to me and 90% how I react to it. And so it is with you...we are in charge of our attitudes."*

I've known Pattie Vargas for more than 18 years and I've watched firsthand the loss and pain she has experienced. I've also witnessed her rise above her circumstances with an attitude of purpose that far outweighs most people's response to adversity. She has redefined what it means to refuse the victim role and choose to have a thriving life and career. You'll be encouraged and inspired by Pattie's story and you, too, will learn keys to navigating your circumstances and living a fulfilling life.

—Pastor Pam Ingold
Family Pastor
The Church at Rancho Bernardo

The Resilience Factor Is Your Superpower

Pattie Vargas

women lead
P U B L I S H I N G™

Family, nothing is more important to me, so this book is for all of you.

Extra special thanks to my amazing husband, Tony, who married *all of us* and continues to be spouse, dad and, now, grandfather to this wonderful and imperfect group of people who do life together.

Are you ready to discover your superpower?

Let's continue to support one another on our Resilience Journey. If you've never written a personal Mission Statement, request my simple, step-by-step template and proclaim your purpose for living. You can register on my website at www.thevargasgroup.net. I look forward to connecting with you!

Table of Contents

Introduction

One day I woke up.

I didn't really want to. I'd felt it coming for a while—although, once I finally woke up, it wasn't exactly *how* I'd expected.

While asleep I could pretend I didn't hear the nagging voice in my head that kept saying, "There must be something more."

I could ignore the hunger for meaning that was gnawing away at my insides, reminding me of the things I once dreamed of doing.

I could pretend I was happy and didn't know, deep down, that I was neglecting some really important things.

Some unspoken part of me knew that if I woke up, I'd have to make some choices. Choices I wasn't ready to make. I'd have to commit to carving out time just for me to explore and pursue things that mattered to me. I would have to take responsibility for my own happiness and fulfillment, and admit that the reason I was not who I wanted to be was—well, my own fault.

Now, in my defense, it's not like I was just sleeping—that would have been a nice luxury. More like I was sleepwalking. My eyes were open; my feet were moving my body forward. I did stuff and functioned like a human being. I was very, very busy with the day-to-day minutiae that fills our lives: in my case, taking care of kids, working a full-time job, going to school, and the activities—geez, the activities!—that seem to be never-ending.

This is what women do. We appear to be an endless reservoir of resources, able to absorb "just one more thing" until infinity. It doesn't occur to us that our energy is limited. We are driven by the need to provide, supply, respond—just be endless "need-meeters." The demands and obligations of life become the life we are living—to the point where we are, literally, sleepwalking through life.

Until we wake up.

I wish we didn't need an *event* to wake us up. It would be nice if our desire would somehow break through the clouds and—shazam!—awaken us, fully aware!

But that's not usually the case. Typically, something happens—job loss, a tragedy involving a loved one, divorce, death, a health scare. Suddenly our life becomes defined by *before* and *after*. We put a point on the timeline and begin to clump our experiences, knowledge, and self-perception on one side or the other. We begin an endless quest for understanding, continually engaging in introspection—often degrading into "woulda-coulda-shoul-das"—until we're weighted down with shame and blame. And because we are so good at feeling responsible for pretty much everything that goes wrong, self-loathing can become our resting place. Put on your "victim" hat, accept your lot in life, and settle in for a long, long, *long* winter.

Unless we wake up!

Because along with the *event*, whatever it may be in your life, comes the possibility of growth. Clarity arrives. The things that matter most become crystal clear, and you begin to see that you—and you alone—can determine how this story ends. The pain is still there—the confusion, the loss, the sense of betrayal, the feeling that life has somehow screwed you over. But you begin to awaken to the idea that you can overcome this. And not just overcome it in order to survive—but overcome it to learn and grow, so you can encourage others to do the same. You can become the person you kept pretending you weren't meant to be. You can serve, give back, and be the light in someone else's darkness.

You see, *the incident* isn't a point on a defined timeline. It's something that happens on the continuum of our life. We have no idea what our future will bring or how long that continuum is. Regardless how we have planned our life, the Universe has a mind of its own—and we must learn the power of resilience, grace, and self-forgiveness to make it through as victors, not victims!

One day I woke up. And yes, an *event* caused it.

And after I got sick of being the victim, I woke up *again*.

And because I know I am not unique, this is *our* story.

Chapter 1

The Wake-Up Call

It was August of 1995, a Saturday. I'd taken a drive to check out a house my husband and I were considering buying to embark on our quest to make money in real estate. He had stayed home with the kids, ages 15, 13, and 9, who were busy doing all the things kids do on a Saturday. I agreed to call him from time to time to check in and discuss the house.

Now, this was before most people had cell phones, so "checking in" meant I had to find a pay phone, pull over, and make the call. Except he didn't answer. I called numerous times, and he never picked up. Annoying—super annoying.

I finally decided to just head home, where I found him sitting in the back patio, drunk and upset. It was decidedly strange for him to be inebriated in the middle of the day—especially when he was the only parent on duty. I asked him what was wrong and…just like that, nothing was ever going to be the same.

He told me he had been seeing someone from work.

The air was sucked out of my universe as I struggled to comprehend words I never expected to hear. These things happen to other people—not me; not us. After all, we'd been married almost 23 years; we had major history together. He'd been the love of my life since I was 15 years old. Not to mention we were up to our eyeballs in debt, we had family responsibilities—and we were Christians, for God's sake!

This can't be happening! I thought.

Then he told me who it was.

Sucker punch to the gut. *You can't be serious.*

Not two weeks earlier he had been complaining to me about her: her work ethic, her loose morals, her mothering techniques. Somehow, something had changed; now she was his "soul mate." To add insult to injury, now that he knew what love really was, he wasn't sure he had *ever* loved *me*.

I'm conditioned to solve problems so, faced with the mother of all problems, I went into solution mode. And because he was accustomed to this, he asked me, "What do we do now?"

"I want you to leave her and stay with us."

We'd been together forever and had children to consider, so I couldn't simply accept that it was all over. But his leaving her was a nonstarter. He said he loved her and couldn't see a life without her in it.

The next week is a blur—yes, just one week. Seven short days later the kids and I were living in another city, where I rented a small condo and enrolled them in a new school.

Why did I leave instead of him? There were lots of reasons—some of them make sense to this day. I worked almost 35 miles away and was concerned about getting home quickly, in the event something happened with one of the kids. Our house was quite large with a lot of landscaping, and I wasn't sure I could maintain it by myself. I didn't have a manual for how to proceed when your world falls apart. The kids and I were all going through our own stages of grief, loss, and mourning, and I was adjusting to a significantly reduced income, smaller living space, and the need to ask for help from time to time.

I found myself defending my ex to our kids in order to maintain some semblance of family status quo—this, despite the reality. One interesting fact came to light, though. Being in a long-term, committed marriage, I just assumed I still loved him. I assumed the character traits I had ascribed to him over the years were accurate. I assumed he was still a decent human being. Big surprise when the realization hit that there was a *big* difference between like and love—and I no longer *liked* him at all.

Chapter 2

The Commitment Curse

Those of us who value commitment, loyalty, and responsibility have a hard time understanding that some ideas or scenarios may be part of our history but have no place in our future. As I reflected on my past, I thought a lot about my love affair with commitment and responsibility.

In 1973, I stood in the church vestibule, my arm linked in my dad's, dressed in an expensive wedding gown, carrying pale blue daisies with baby's breath, and trailing a long veil. The pews were packed, all eyes turned toward me. "Color My World" was my cue to enter as my fiancé waited at the altar in a champagne and black tux. This was my big day! I'd turned 19 two weeks before, and I was ready to begin my new life as a married woman!

And then my dad squeezed my arm, turned to me and said, "It's not too late to back out."

Now, that was one of those lightbulb moments we only recognize in hindsight. In the grand scheme of things, if I had taken him up on that offer, the world would not have ended. But at that moment? Was he kidding? I poked him and said, "Come on, everyone's watching. Let's go!"

That little exchange pretty much summed up the next twenty-plus years of my life. It was always "too late" to turn back now. If I committed to something, by God, I followed through. Warning signs could pop up all over the place, but I firmly believed in staying the course, even if it led me right off the edge.

How can commitment be a curse? If anything, it seems like we need *more* people with the moral fortitude to make a vow and stick with it. But just because we've made a commitment to something doesn't mean it's set in stone—or that our feet are encased in concrete. If we're honest, many of the decisions and commitments made over the course of our lives fall into the category of "Seemed Like a Good Idea at the Time." But that internal drive to see it through—no matter what—can be a hard habit to break!

I know people who have overstayed their welcome in a job because it was comfortable or easy. They got attached to the benefits, commute, or other perks—while relevance passed them by. It's a balancing act, for sure, to understand when it's better for your career to follow a new technology or when the current demands of your family life require you to slow down.

Often we stay in relationships for similar reasons or because we fear the unknown, even when we know the relationship isn't healthy for us—or anyone else, for that matter. Or we stay the course on the major we selected in school even though it's boring us to tears, and we know we will never be happy in that profession. We say to ourselves, "I have invested so much already" or "it's too late to turn back now." We revisit these excuses many years later when we realize that we're living the results of those decisions—or nondecisions, as it were.

A sense of obligation can cause us to turn a blind eye to reality and view a situation through the lens of what we wish it could be, not how it truly is. Having a long-term marriage come to an abrupt end has convinced me how powerfully deceptive that lens can be. Sometimes a change is needed. But taking a new direction requires careful consideration. You have to weigh all the impacts before making a move. The more difficult the change or far-reaching the impact, the more you should seek the insight and input of some trusted advisors.

Deviating from course disrupts our sense of order. For me, personally, that need for order can be a wicked, *wicked* taskmaster. It has taken decades of introspection to convince myself it is not only OK, but really healthy, to disrupt the order of things! At the risk of revealing how ridiculously anal-retentive I've been over the course of my life, let me share with you some of the things I now allow to get interrupted or disordered:

1. If I'm reading a book and not enjoying it much, it's OK to abandon the book.

2. If my house is dirty but I'd rather go out with friends, it's OK to put play before work.

3. If someone sends me an email marked "urgent," it's OK to respond at my convenience.

4. If I spent more than I should have for an article of clothing and then realized I really don't like it, it's OK to recycle.

5. If I'm sick, the world is not going to end if I stay home from work, from a meeting, from a party.

6. If I'm making a presentation and suddenly realize even I don't believe what I'm saying, it's OK to take it in another direction.

7. If I want dinner for breakfast, or breakfast for dinner, it's OK!

8. Here are a couple of big ones—healthy lifestyle changes don't have to wait for Monday, and New Year's resolutions can be made any time!

I love this quote by Steve Maraboli, "Why let go of yesterday? Because yesterday has already let go of *you*." What this says to me is that it is OK—and actually wise—to reevaluate once in a while whether something is still working for me. Am I still challenged by my work? If not, let go. Has compromise crept into my relationships? Have my more important commitments gone stale? If so, let go.

Chapter 3

Is My Personal GPS Working?

Unless you want to constantly second-guess yourself or make decisions on the fly with no idea whether they are right or wrong for you, it's a good idea to identify what you believe in and what you stand for. Call it your personal mission statement, your platform of belief, your internal GPS, whatever: knowing what you value and being incredibly intentional about who you are brings you back on course when you get sidetracked. And, friends—when you're in the midst of a battle, it's a tough time to figure out your life strategy.

The problem is, if we don't define ourselves ahead of time, it's tempting for an event, a point in time, a "fork in the road," if you will, to characterize our lives as "before" and "after." It's incredibly easy to lose perspective, become hyper-focused on what has happened, and miss the lesson we could learn from it. And if we fail to learn, what's the point?

The good thing about adversity is that it gives us the opportunity to discover hidden or forgotten truths about ourselves. But that's not a given, my friends. You really *could* die in the wilderness—this could be the thing that completely takes you out! What makes the difference between going over or going under? Well, I define it as "The Resilience Factor"—the thing within us that lets us choose to be someone who overcomes, not a victim.

Our cars come with this fabulous thing called a GPS—you tell it where you want to go, and it maps out a route for you! It even offers alternatives if there is traffic or an accident ahead that could affect your ability to get where you're going. Of course, you could ignore the GPS and just wing it, figuring somehow things will work out in your favor and you will end up in a good place. That's a great way to end up hopelessly lost, out of money, with no one to come to your rescue! A good directional system seems like a much better idea.

The things we say we value are what make up our personal GPS. Those values might include things like honesty, integrity, our health, our family—the key is, they are the values *we* have chosen as important. They represent who we are, what we stand for, how we lead our lives. My value system had become completely overshadowed by my husband's—when he had a perspective I disagreed with, I didn't speak up…somehow, nothing seemed that important. Until one day, in front of our children, he voiced an opinion *as fact* that was just so wrong, so opposite of everything I knew to be right, I had to say something. The point of view he expressed offended me to my very core, and I woke up to the fact that my failure to speak up meant I was modeling compliance.

My principles were buried. I was not intentional about anything—and shame on me. An old military adage says, "If you want to defeat them, distract them." I'd gotten distracted, sidetracked—I was basically sleepwalking through life, preoccupied with the day-to-day hassles and the busyness of my days. Somehow, along the way, I lost who I was.

Imagine I'm holding an egg in my hand. Just by looking at it, you can't tell if it is hard-boiled or raw and, unless it's coming right at you, you probably don't care! But if this egg represents my value system, that's a different thing. Some values can be compromised with minimal impact—they aren't high on the "life or death" spectrum. They may be somewhat important, but they aren't going to change the direction of my life one way or another. So it's OK if I'm a little careless with my egg—if I neglect this value.

The problem was…my egg represented how I raised my kids. How I felt about human rights and dignity. My tolerance level for bigotry and racism. My relationship with my God. And I was careless with all of them! I tossed this egg around like I was certain it was hard-boiled and, in the process, left a lot of messes behind me. Contrary to popular belief, sometimes you can't put Humpty-Dumpty back together again.

So, yes, some things can be compromised. But without giving it some thought, without having those values questioned and tried, how would you know? If you haven't at least contemplated the impact of losing something, how can you know how much it would matter? I was forced to acknowledge that by not defending my values—by not standing up for things that were sacred to me—I was essentially agreeing they weren't all that important. I gave tacit approval for those offensive opinions, beliefs, and bias to be verbalized—with no reprisal. Like it or not, I was *aligned* with them.

Knowing your values—being intentional about who you are and what you stand for—brings you back on track. When you're in the midst of the fight, it's your North Star, your benchmark to look back to. If you have never taken the time to draft your own personal Mission Statement or Platform of Belief, I encourage you to do so. Find a quiet place with a nice cup of coffee or a glass of wine, and get in touch with what matters the most to you. I wrote mine as I was navigating my way through the end of my marriage, and it remains framed on my desktop to this day.

This I Believe

I want to live my life in such a manner that being in relationship with me enriches others.

I believe in and support the rights and freedoms of my country but also recognize and value the personal responsibility that goes along with living in a democratic society.

I value resilience and have determined to teach my children and others that no one can make you a victim without your permission.

I am self-motivated, knowing I am owed nothing, nor can I expect others to create my future and fortunes.

I desire to bring honor to my family, my community, and my God in all that I do.

A.J. Muste (1885-1967) was one of the leading nonviolent social activists of his time, eventually committing his time and energies to peaceful war resistance and civil rights. During the Vietnam War he conducted a solitary, nightly candlelight vigil in front of the White House. One night, a reporter asked him, derisively, "Do you really think you are going to change the policies of this country by standing out here alone at night with a candle?" Muste replied, "Oh, I don't do it to change the country. I do it so the country *won't change me.*"

Friends, that's what having your actions and decisions in alignment with your value system looks like. The way we live our lives, the way we show up on a daily basis, the things we *tolerate,* are determined by the things we say matter the most. When difficulties come, you know who you are and what you stand for.

1995

I am in a state of flux, not even *re*-defining myself.
I'm defining myself for the very first time.

For more than half my life I was your other half.
Hooked up with you when I was too young to know who I was
and hooked too deep by the time I began to wonder if there
was something more.

I am learning things about myself I never knew before.
Some are things others always told me and some are things that
probably only I can understand the significance of.

It's hard to know who I am or the kind of person I am when
one minute I feel strong and capable and very good at what I
do, and the next feel as fragile and needy as a child.
My emotions are worn raw swinging as they do from angst to
confidence to euphoria…and then all back again.

I need to know who I am!
I can't make the same mistakes again and yet—what makes me
so different now?

I don't want to need anyone—I want to feel like I am enough
in myself and by myself.
And yet, I feel sorry for people who are alone and live alone
and sleep alone.
But still—even sorrier for people who are married forever and
have nothing to say to each other,
nothing in common but…being married.

So who the hell am I and what do I want?

I know this: whatever it is that I want must come from *me*.

It can't come from a man or from my family or from a learned value system.

It must come from the definition I build within myself.
This is no new-age revelation.
This is common sense, hold-ya-together-when-it-all-goes-to-hell sensibility.

Never had it. Gotta get it. Gonna find it.

—Pattie Vargas, 1995

Chapter 4

The Inner Circle

I tend to collect friends and hang onto them way too long. Our Inner Circle should be sacred– we should guard it like a precious garden and allow in only the people who are on our journey *with* us. It was a difficult thing to learn that not all of my friends were enthralled with my newfound sense of self-worth or my decision to act in my best interest. Hardest of all was to realize that some of them had their own agendas for my life and, if I chose *not* to follow their path, it might mean the end of our friendship. Allow me to introduce you to these characters.

The Victimizer

When my marriage first broke up, my girlfriends and family clustered around me. Even some people I only knew through work became suddenly close and caring. It was gratifying and comforting to be surrounded with such support and love.

For a while.

The first few weeks I was, more or less, a basket case. I held it together for my kids, and I kept moving forward, making plans, and resolving issues. But there were lots of tears, lots of hand-wringing, lots of freaking out with close friends. This type of behavior on my part attracted a certain kind of attention: I came to refer to these folks as the Victimizers. They would sympathize with me, decree that my life was pretty much over, make comments that clearly indicated I would never recover from this one moment of time in my life. The conversation was always about losing—what had been "stolen from me"—and how unfair life was in general, with no redemption in sight.

While the Victimizers were reducing me to nothing more than the butt end of life's cruel joke, they were elevating themselves to the role of caretaker. This was their opportunity to take over my life, make key decisions, and mold me into what they thought was best for me. I was their latest project! Well, as much fun as it was to have someone who willingly listened to my every complaint, I was, after all, a grown-ass woman, and I needed to find *my* way in *my new normal.*

Does this sound familiar, friend? Is this happening to you right now?

As appealing as it is to listen as your friends list every injustice done to you by life, circumstance, or other people, you must resist the urge to jump into that mudhole with them. If you stay there too long, it becomes your permanent address. I've met women whose marriage broke up years and years ago, and they still can provide every detail and recall the pain as if it had happened yesterday. Their life ended the day he walked out.

They allowed that one event to become the defining moment, not just of their life, but of themselves.

I have a coaching client who, during our first session, spent a considerable amount of time talking about his layoff from a corporate job *12 years previously*. Despite being a talented individual with a desirable skill set who found new employment relatively quickly, he constantly referred back to the mistreatment he received at the hands of that previous employer. He was stuck in a victim mindset and allowed it to define him! He was in frequent contact with coworkers from that time who had been let go when he was. They got together for happy hour (or in their case, *un*happy hour!) and talked about who was still with the company, who was getting screwed, and about all the people responsible for the chaos and mayhem. These colleagues were both Victims and Victimizers, and their solidarity was a never-ending, vicious cycle of bitterness.

Why was he unable to move on from that experience? His reasons were unique to him. For me, it was the sudden unmooring from everything I knew, the loss of all the things that connected me to my life:

- **Loss of Identity:** When our image of ourselves is tied up in the job we do, the friends we have, our spouse and/or children, any disruption to that situation can lead to an identity crisis. Our worth is determined by how well we perform, our reputation in the organization or community, or the attention our role generates. We belong to a unique "club" made up of others who are just like us—and when we are suddenly kicked out of that club, where do we fit in?

I enjoyed being married. I loved the friends we had and the comfortable camaraderie I had with other couples who understood the challenges, benefits, and joys of marriage. I also appreciated having three relatively normal kids, and the kinship I felt with other parents when discussing the trials and tribulations of each stage of parenting. This was a large part of my identity, and when I was suddenly single, it made many of my married friends uncomfortable. Maybe they felt divorce was contagious, or perhaps they were afraid of facing issues in their own relationships. Whatever the reason, the invitations slowed down, and I found myself gravitating toward other single moms—a new club.

I also experienced a change in some of my professional relationships with married men. I had great rapport with many of the men I worked with, and enjoyed our collaboration and fun interactions—until I was single. A number of them backed away, no longer willing to work one-on-one with me, afraid of what it would "look like" or what their "wives would think." Apparently working closely with a married woman was "safe" but, now that I was single, "something might happen." Interesting rationale. Based on my experience, I wouldn't consider marriage a guaranteed deterrent to adultery.

- **Loss of Purpose:** I was on a particular road. I had a five-year plan. I knew what my primary role in life was.

Then, suddenly, none of that existed anymore.

Most of us are planners to some extent—even if we don't have a formal, strategic blueprint, we have a pretty good idea where we want to be in five years and some thoughts on how to make that happen. When the plan changes, we find ourselves adrift.

When my marriage ended, we had just completed a large addition to our home financed with a second mortgage. We were also in the process of buying a second home about 25 miles away to move our kids into a better school system and rent the first house for income. I had gone back to school to improve my chances of finding a better job, and my husband was always busy with home improvement projects to increase the value of our house.

In other words, we had plans—plans completely upended by my new priorities. Instead of expanding our "property empire," I had to find an apartment I could afford and put my education on hold for a while; no job change for me in the near future.

- **Loss of Perspective:** When I looked at my entire life through the lens of this one event, my perspective became very, very narrow. I couldn't see this as one point on the timeline—every decision I made and every thought I entertained was filtered through my perception of loss. Perception can be brutal. I've seen beautiful, accomplished women embark on a series of self-improvement initiatives because they believed they were no longer smart or attractive. Following a job loss, people can experience a complete crisis of competence, even when the loss is not performance-related but the result of a reorganization. We can assume unwarranted guilt following the loss of a loved one, beating ourselves up for not doing enough.

I found writing very cathartic during this time. Sometimes just writing down my pinpoint perspective made me see how shortsighted I was. I also read inspirational writings of other women who had "come through" to the other side. You need someone alongside to encourage you when you can't see the forest for the trees.

Which leads me back to the Victimizer. You will likely experience one or all of the losses above at some point in your life, and this is like blood in the water to a Victimizer. The sooner you recognize their behavior, the easier it will be to manage. In defense of Victimizers, their intent likely isn't meant to keep you down. Some of them are natural-born caretakers and problem-solvers, and can't resist the urge to take over your life. They may love you dearly and be heartbroken for you. Your job is to regain control by limiting your exposure to their negative view of life. It doesn't have to signify the end of your friendship; but if it does, you're probably better off.

No Victims

You're dealt a hand and you play it.
Sometimes you win, sometimes you lose.

Sometimes you make a dumb play and can recover from it!
But sometimes you're not so lucky, and it's a fatal move—
game over.

Either way, you're nobody's victim.
You held the cards, and *you* made the plays.
Maybe you were playing with a cheater, someone who bent the
rules and slid the cards in and out at will.
But when you find out he's a liar, you end the game.

Move on, start another game; different players, a different hand.
Another chance to win, or at least break even.

No victims. You're in charge. You choose.

—Pattie Vargas, 1995

The Accuser

There's a special kind of person who loves to blame the
"victim," a word I use with great hesitation. They're the ones
who say, "She must have asked for it" or "You shouldn't have
been there in the first place" or any other number of useless,
uninformed and, certainly, unwanted opinions. The Accusers'
compulsion to share their opinion seems to be in direct correlation to how unhelpful it is!

As word got out that my marriage was ending, I saw a different side to some individuals who had been part of my Inner Circle. I came to refer to them, not so fondly, as the Accusers. In their view of the world, surely *I* caused my situation. Their accusations raised feelings ranging from *that's crazy* to *OK, maybe they're right,* and often had the desired effect of making me second-guess myself and take on the blame. Assigning blame doesn't really get us anywhere, whether the blame fell on him or on me. But to have so-called friends jump on the "Let's blame Pattie" bandwagon and point out everything they had apparently been storing up for years came out of left field. Their accusations sounded something like this:

"You should have seen this coming—we did."

OK, if they saw it coming and cared about me, why didn't they say something? Because, in reality, they didn't. Some people just have to appear superior and all-knowing, even at your expense. For one, brief moment, they have one-upped you. And what does that say about your relationship with them? I came to understand that, on some level, they were jealous of me and what I had, and my misfortune signified the *best day ever* for them. These kinds of friends we can all live without.

"What did you do? You must have done *something* to drive him away!"

Ouch. This hurt most of all because there was likely an element of truth buried deep in that pile of manure. This rationale comes from a fear that if it happened to you, it could happen to me, and we just don't like to think that way. After all, in the

American Dream, we are all in control of our destiny, and nothing bad will ever happen to us, right?

Psychologists refer to this mentality as the "Just World Hypothesis." It's the assumption we all deserve our outcomes or consequences. If you do good things—or the "right" things—only good things will happen to you. If something unfortunate or unthinkable happens…well, you must have messed up somewhere along the line. The result is *just*—it's *fair*. People who subscribe to this reasoning, I believe, are frightened by their own vulnerability. Their view of the world as a safe place where they are in control is threatened, so in an attempt to regain control, they blame the victim. If they accepted the idea that misfortune can be random, they would need to face the fact that they, too, could lose their marriage, their child, their life savings, their job.

I came to understand this variety of accusers more than the "know-it-alls" because I, too, had fallen into that trap. I remember clearly, before I had children, making comments like "My kid will never…" (fill in the blank). Quite humbling to look back and realize that, yes, they will. They did. And then some. And of course, I never conceived the possibility of my marriage ending. We were special—we did things "right." If we're honest, I think we have all been highly judgmental of someone else's loss until it happens to us. Adversity is the great equalizer.

Accusers have a driving need to explain suffering. Like Job's "friends," who insisted he was being punished for his sins, Accusers simply cannot accept that Some. Things. Just. Are. There has to be an explanation and, in their extreme wisdom, they defend God by dispensing some useless piece of commentary. In response to the death of a loved one, for example, they suggest, "Heaven needed him more than you did." That's the stupidest response to death I've ever heard. Somehow, I don't think God needs any of us defending His actions. And to think we have an explanation for everything that happens is, frankly, the very definition of hubris. "Everything happens for a reason" is another infuriating judgment we could all do without. Why do bad things happen to good people? Well, they could just as easily ask, why do good things happen to bad people? The truth is, I don't know. And neither do they.

If we don't protect our hearts and minds from these accusations, we are fair game for the Victimizers, who often swoop in right behind the Accusers to help you lick your wounds. Pretty soon we can find ourselves in a vicious cycle of blame and shame. It is *our* responsibility—our responsibility—to rise above our circumstance and reject the victim mindset. We're the only ones who can write the end to our own story.

Some Other Unhelpful People

The Victimizer and the Accuser were not the only unhelpful people in my rodeo. *Au contraire.* Remember me mentioning that I had gotten distracted by life? That I wasn't being intentional about my belief system? That pretty much meant the gates were down, and I was collecting friends right and left—some good for me, and some not so good for me. Here are a couple more. See if you're hanging out with these folks.

The Tempter

In the early days of my singlehood, I was pretty determined I wanted nothing more to do with men. I had no confidence in my ability to make wise choices and, besides, I had a lot on my plate. I was also fully on the "Blame the Victim (Me)" bandwagon. I knew I was fat, unattractive, old, and unlovable, so no need to even worry about dating.

In my quest for self-awareness and to answer the endless "How did this happen to me?" questions, I was reading a lot of female authors, from early trailblazers of the feminist movement to faith-based thought leaders and new-age-mama enlightenment. Much of it was wonderful and expanded my thinking, helping me realize how little I had questioned over the years and what a narrow perspective I had of the world. I am so grateful for the women writers who had gone before me and were willing to share their experiences and journey; their wisdom and transparency helped me determine my value and regain my purpose.

Some of it, though, was downright self-serving. It painted women as bitter and angry at not having the same "rights" as men—meaning the "right" to sleep with anyone they wanted, married, single, whatever.

Do not get me wrong. I am a proud feminist. I am an advocate for equal pay, equal rights, workplace equity, rightful distribution of earned marital assets, etc. I believe we need more women in government to bring about a more collaborative, reasoned approach to lawmaking and put an end to chest-thumping, butt-waving, feces-throwing political discourse.

But in the litany of the "rights" that are afforded men and not women, the right to engage in indiscriminate sex isn't one I want or need. If this is your lifestyle choice, by all means go for it, but don't call it a feminist issue. A few women in my circle banged this drum relentlessly and felt the need to enlighten me. Their rationale sounded something like this, "You've been cooped up for years and years! It's about time you got this party started. After all, *what did being good and loyal get you?*"

Their reasoning was bizarre. And to shroud it in a "what's good for the goose is good for the gander" justification completely missed the issue of a personal value system. Men and women both have to answer to an individual code of conduct; it's not a matter of equality at all.

Society tends to be more accepting of a serial womanizer than it is of a woman who "sleeps around" (that is the gentle term— we all know the other one). But each individual, male or female, has to look themselves in the eye at the end of the day and be comfortable with their choices. These Tempters claimed their right to "act like men," apparently without considering why they would want to.

So, speaking of men…I would be remiss if I didn't include them in the cast of characters who made an appearance in those early days. At the time of my divorce I worked in information technology, a male-dominated world. I had a lot of male friends, and many of them were wonderfully supportive—so much so that I married one of them a few years later. We've now been married for more than 20 years. But there were others. I shall refer to them as:

The Temporary Replacements

These guys had the biggest hearts—all they wanted to do was "fill the void" that surely existed, and each was completely convinced he was the man for the job. I hope you sense the sarcasm. The first one to appear was an obnoxious coworker I could barely stand to be around; our interactions had never been anything more than mutually tolerant at best. That didn't stop him, though, from sending me an email (at work, no less) notifying me that if I ever felt lonely and needed "someone to hold me," he would be my guy! His offer was so outrageously hilarious I wasn't even offended. I forwarded it to three or four of my closest girlfriends, and we had a good laugh at his expense. (Hey, don't send an email you don't want forwarded!)

Another guy at work also offered his "services," as a counselor of sorts. He was a senior leader in the company—my boss's boss, no less, and several levels above me—so his actions were completely inappropriate. He called me into his office one afternoon, closed the door, and offered me a seat on his couch (can you say *Mad Men?*). He told me he knew I was going through a divorce (I had not shared that with him), and he wanted to assure me it had nothing to do with my attractiveness or lack thereof. "You see," he counseled, "men are just not made to be monogamous." Did I mention he was married with three children?

Did these men think so highly of themselves—or was I tele-graphing how little I thought of myself? The answer is yes—and yes. They did think highly of themselves, and I definitely was giving off the no-confidence vibe. I had unknowingly fallen into the phenomenon of the Players in Pursuit of the

Vulnerable Separated Woman. Yep, this is a thing, and almost every newly single woman I've coached has had this experience. The men who play this game will be assessing you on three factors:

- **A Low (or out-of-practice) Bullshit Meter.** The Replacement is counting on your vulnerability. If you've been in a lengthy relationship, possibly it's been quite a while since a man called you beautiful, desirable, smart, or (fill in the blank), and they know you will drink it in like rain on parched ground. They are the best listeners: they encourage your confidences, then reward you with everything you want to hear. They will entice you with whatever was missing in your last relationship and understand you like no one ever has!

- **Level of Sexual Frustration.** If your relationship was stale before it ended, you might be feeling a little frustrated. After all, you probably weren't getting much—or any—before the relationship ended, and you sure aren't getting any now. The Replacement will try to convince you that he, and he alone, knows how to please you, and his only concern is your satisfaction. He doesn't refer to sex as much as he talks about romance, and he will assure you that foreplay is his favorite part of the act.

- **No Strings Attached.** Since you are only separated and not technically available, you're not looking to get married right now. Besides, you probably have a few kids and the accompanying responsibilities that go with that. The Replacement sees this as Fair Game with No Strings

> Attached, unless he hangs on a little too long. Then you
> will see him disappear in a flash, usually with excuses like
> "you are still finding yourself" or "your kids are your
> priority" or other justifications that put the onus on you.

As I write this, I can feel the self-loathing and disgust rising—I
can't believe I actually fell for some of this. But I learned to
forgive myself over time. After all, I hadn't had a new relationship since I was 15 years old, so I guess I was entitled to a few
mistakes. These experiences were helpful on my journey; each
time I encountered behavior like this, I learned something new,
and I gained strength inside. I came to understand that, buried
or not, I *did* have a strong sense of right and wrong, just and
unjust, good and bad. Every misguided man who thought I
needed his brand of rescuing served as a guideline to a better
definition of the kind of relationship I deserved.

Tough
Tough
was your mother's word
for the kind of woman
she didn't want you
to become, someone
who didn't know her place,
who didn't know the game
rules, or even worse, broke
them all, went after
what she wanted
openly, instead of playing
spider, leaving a web

that glittered innocence,
catching the morning
dew, the unwary
fly in the same
sticky threads,
surprised.

But you know tough
is the rock that takes
the water over and over,
becoming grooved but still
distinctly itself, the roots of
morning glories, honeysuckle,
that persevere and nurture
blossoms, Queen Anne's lace
and chicory that keep on
coming back in the haze
of the highway,
in torn-up building sites,
burnt-out lots, resilient,
tough.

—Edwina Trentham [1]

The Champion

I've let you in on some of the folks who shouldn't have been
inside my Inner Circle. In turn, you've probably identified some
people in your life who probably should go. I encourage you to
follow through on those inner warnings. If your "friends" aren't
with you on your journey to transformation, they will only hold
you back. You will find yourself confused by their counsel and

sidetracked by *their* ideas of how *you* ought to live *your* life. If they're worth keeping around, they will listen to your feedback and adjust their behavior. If not, they have given you a valuable gift: cut them loose and move on.

Thankfully there was another kind of person in my Inner Circle—many of them, in fact. I came to call them my Champions. They were the ones who were there when it was inconvenient, when it cost them something to be my friend, when they sensed a derailment in my future. Champions didn't just say nice things and take my side. Sometimes they pointed out where I was messing up and compromising myself. What set The Champions apart was their steadfast belief in my ability to rise above, to become the person I was meant to be, and their refusal to let me tear myself down. Whenever I spent time with a Champion, I came away with clarity and confidence—whether my problems had been solved or not. I was able to believe in myself because they believed in me.

The investment of time, energy, and love that each of my Champions devoted to me continues to pay dividends. Their example was one I wanted to emulate with friends and family, and eventually led to the mission for my coaching business: the desire to invest in guiding others to their better, new normal. My Champions were there to:

- **Listen without judgment.** If I expressed a new idea, a fresh perspective, a possible career change, they just listened. Often I didn't want their input or guidance, just for them to be a sounding board. They knew there would be time to support or intervene if the idea became real.

- **Change the channel.** If they sensed I was going down a rabbit hole of self-loathing and despair, they redirected the story. They reminded me of the good things I was doing and the smart decisions I'd already made. They demonstrated their unwavering belief in me.

- **Anticipate a downfall.** A few of my Champions took it upon themselves to keep me busy in those early days. If they knew I was going to be alone, someone showed up out of the blue to take me to a movie, out for a drink, or to go for a bike ride.

- **Tell me the hard truth.** When someone truly loves you, they are not afraid to tell you when you're making a mistake. I nearly made a very bad decision born out of panic and fear. I am eternally grateful to the friend who pointed out the close parallels in the life I was considering and the life I had just left, bringing me clarity and wisdom.

Pay it forward. Be a Champion in someone else's life. You will find it the most rewarding role you ever play.

Chapter 5

How Do I Turn Off The Voices In My Head?

I t was a relief to learn I wasn't the only one with a little voice in my head that never ran out of things it thought I needed to hear. As I gained the courage to challenge that voice, I learned that everyone suffers from this. I'm not alone!

Most of the time it isn't just one voice. It's a chorus, a choir, a committee that seems to be on a mission to destroy my self-confidence. Where do these voices come from, and how do I turn them off?

First let's take a look at where they originate. We all come to adulthood with a boatload of personal history—past experiences, cultural norms, family background—that combines to make up our mental programming. Often unconsciously, we allow these inputs to condition us into a way of being that forms our personal bias, views, and preconceptions. In a nutshell, this is our view of the world: the good, the bad, and the ugly.

This platform gives birth to thoughts (or the voice in the head) that feed into our feelings. The voice in the head says, "You never finish anything," and you feel like a failure. You mentally review every unfinished project, commitment, promise you've ever made throughout your life. The more you review, the more the feeling is reinforced, and the more real the narrative becomes.

And then what? Our feelings drive the actions we take—or don't take. If it's true that I never finish anything, I'm not likely to act on that new idea I have. After all, it will become yet another thing I tried and gave up on. I'll end up feeling even worse about myself. The end result? If I'm afraid to try something new, I stay stuck right where I am. And it all started with a voice telling me, "You never finish anything."

Thoughts become feelings.

Feelings drive actions.

Actions beget results.

Where did I get the idea I never finish anything? Along the way I'm sure I finished *something*, right? Homework assignments were completed and turned in. Parties were planned and given. I got pregnant and gave birth so, clearly, I finished *that*. But at some point in time, someone made the accusation, and it related to something important enough that I took it in and made it part of the narrative.

The first time I believed I was fat was in second grade. I'm sure it stemmed from an innocent comment, but, unfortunately, it came from someone whose opinion mattered a great deal to me. So at the tender age of seven or eight, I accepted that I was fat and made it part of my story. From then on, it wasn't hard to find evidence that reinforced this belief. It didn't help that my name rhymed with "fatty" and that kids loved that kind of schoolyard taunt.

Every outfit that was too snug, every boy who didn't like me back, every friend I had who was even slightly thinner than me was a constant reminder that "I. Was. Fat." And that thought led to deeply entrenched feelings of self-loathing, unattractiveness, uncertainty, and a lack of confidence in my own self-worth. I used to look at girls who were heavier than me, yet seemed so self-assured, and wonder why? How could they be so happy and confident when they looked like *that*? My sense of self was completely—unhealthily so—wrapped up in my perceived "fattiness."

You can probably imagine the actions those feelings drove. Name a diet, I've been on it. There isn't a "get thin quick" pill I haven't taken. And when the results were slow to come or success was short-lived, the cycle would begin again. It really didn't matter how unrealistic my expectations were, or how distorted my self-perception was. "I am fat" became my reality.

Results are at the end of the "thoughts, feelings, actions" sequence. They are the *visible symptoms* of the root cause. If you want a different result, you have to go back to the beginning of the sequence—your thoughts. Too often we focus on taking a different action. We tell ourselves we're going to stop doing the things that create results we don't like! But you can't stop doing what you're doing without challenging the thought that gave birth to the feeling that drove the action.

I want to make a clear distinction between *Results* and *Circumstances*. The changes in our lives, such as the death of a loved one, the cancer diagnosis, the reduction in force, aging, the end of a marriage—those are all Circumstances, not Results. Results come about from actions we take that are driven by our thoughts and feelings. We did not cause the Circumstance and can't control that it happened—but we can control how we think, feel, and act—and have a direct impact on the results we experience.

It's hard to change. If it were easy, the self-help market wouldn't exist. One way to change the thought—the voice in the head—is to refuse to *give* it a voice. Most of what is spitballing around in our head simply isn't true. But when we speak the thoughts out loud, we are agreeing with them. We are validating that "yes, I am fat." "Yes, I never finish anything." "I'm too old to start a new career." "I'll never be financially secure."

When we buy in to the lies, we create an environment where possibility no longer exists. We become isolated from truth and reality—and *nothing good comes from isolation.* Isolation kills hope. Perspective dies in isolation. Trying to manage the voices in our head by ourselves, with no additional input, is difficult. Perspective comes from stepping back and seeing the bigger picture, and this often requires the help of others. Here's a time-tested credo: *The banana that leaves the bunch gets skinned.*

When I was suddenly single, I learned the benefit of having a strong, dissenting voice to challenge the lies I was giving voice to. One day as I was listing all the things that were wrong with me—and doing an excellent job of making the case for what a loser I was—one of my Champions stopped me with this: "Wait a minute. I'm a pretty awesome person. And if I'm such an awesome person, why would I be hanging around with some-one as useless as you?" Stopped me cold. Her indignation was so unexpected that pretty soon we were laughing. My litany of complaints seemed so ludicrous in that context.

The less we give voice to the thought, the less power it has. When we refrain from repeating the lie or, better yet, challenge it with a more realistic, positive version, we take control of the narrative. I'm not talking about baseless positivity—that doesn't help reframe the story. I prefer a healthy dose of reality with a pinch of humor. That's how change begins. And the more intentional we are about breaking the cycle, the more powerful we become.

It's important to note that some of the thoughts in our head are good ones. These are strong, positive thoughts that speak to our character, like "stealing is wrong" or "everyone deserves respect." By all means, give voice to these thoughts. Ironically, the more you challenge the negative voices in your head, the stronger the good ones become.

Mood Swings

I'm a great big bundle of hormones, I am.

Blame it on something, can't be Just Because.

It's the moon, it's the weather, it's cuz you're a damn woman.

Can't be because everyone around me is suffering from chronic
insensitivity.
Naw, gotta be my fault,
swinging from extreme to extreme
from joy to despair
from love to hate
from more than enough to barely adequate.

Hide the weapons, hide the liquor
(hide the ice cream or she'll balloon herself to death)
we'd never get her carcass out the door, what are we to do?

wait it out, hormones level off
full moons pass
she'll get over it

(but you're all still here!)

—Pattie Vargas, 1996

Chapter 6

Forgiving
Is Not Forgetting

When a life-altering change implodes our life plan and we struggle through the ensuing chaos, it's hard to see what could lie beyond. Circumstances challenge our self-perception and, if we aren't mindful, the change can begin to define us. We can become prisoners of our past. Remember, the things we go through are meant to be lessons, not life sentences.

Refusing to forgive can impose that life sentence. Forgiveness is hard; I won't deny that. Especially when the impact of even a point-in-time event can have a long-lasting ripple effect. It would be so easy if we could simply say the words, "I forgive you," and walk away with our memory erased and the path before us cleared of all debris. (Remember the "neuralyzer" in the movie *Men in Black*? How I *wish* that really existed!)

I think we sometimes confuse forgiveness with reconciliation. Forgiveness is one-way. It doesn't require the other party to understand or even know about it. Reconciliation is two-way. Both parties come together with a desire to heal the relationship and find a way forward. In my case, reconciliation was pretty much out of the question, especially since I had an aversion to my husband having a girlfriend. But I had to forgive unless I wanted to be controlled by hurt, anger, and the need for revenge. There's an old saying, "Unforgiveness is like consuming poison and waiting for the other person to die." If I wanted to move on, to learn and grow, forgiveness was a requirement. Ugh! But how?

In 2000, I met Dr. Edie Eger, and that encounter was one of those life-changing, serendipitous experiences. Dr. Edie is a Holocaust survivor. She entered Auschwitz in 1944 with her sister, Magda, and her parents. Her parents were directed to the left; she and Magda to the right. She didn't know that would be the last time she saw her mother and father.

Edie was a ballerina and, as other artists and performers were forced to do, she was often summoned to dance before Dr. Josef Mengele, the Angel of Death. Can you imagine such a thing? When she danced, she closed her eyes and imagined the music was Tchaikovsky and she was dancing "Romeo and Juliet" in the Budapest opera house. When the Americans marched into Auschwitz to liberate the prisoners, Edie weighed 40 pounds, her back was broken, and she was lying on top of a garbage pile where her tormentors had tossed her and left her for dead. One of the soldiers noticed her hand moving and rescued her; that small, defiant wave of the hand saved her life.

Among the many life lessons Edie shared with me was that forgiveness was a decision she made. If she lived her life with bitterness, Hitler would have had the ultimate revenge. She didn't want to be viewed as damaged goods, and she didn't want to be defined by what had happened to her. Her life was going to count for something. And so it has. She has lived to see her great-grandchildren and has a thriving practice as a clinical psychologist, an expert in helping others through post-traumatic stress disorder. Edie believes most of the limitations in our lives are self-imposed. My favorite saying of hers is, "The greatest concentration camp is in your mind, and the key is in your pocket."

How could I hold onto unforgiveness when confronted with this kind of courage? I am privileged to have met Edie when I did, and I have learned so much from her life. But forgiving someone isn't "one-and-done." It's a three-step process:

1. **Acknowledge the damage done to you.** The offense was real: no amount of positive spin will diminish that it happened, that it hurt, that it left a scar on your soul.

2. **Choose to release the debt you feel is owed.** That choosing part is key: this is a crossroads where the outcome can go one way or another. Refusing to release the debt equates to a need for revenge.

3. **Remember your decision as often as needed.** Yep. Just doing steps one and two doesn't erase the ripple effect of the damage done. Every time you are confronted with the reality that exists because of the offense, you have to make the choice all over again. Fortunately, with time, this gets easier.

One final thought on forgiving…it's not forgetting. And that's a good thing. If we don't want to repeat the mistakes we've made in the past, we have to remember what led to them. It's been said, "The definition of insanity is doing the same thing over and over and expecting a different outcome." We may forgive the spouse who was unfaithful, but we make different choices in our future partners or in the way we live our lives with them. We may forgive the business partner who stole our clients and more than his or her fair share of the profits, but we will put safeguards into place to protect ourselves legally in the future. Remembering the wrongdoing doesn't mean we haven't forgiven; it might just be a good indicator that we are learning.

Chapter 7

Returning To
My Original Form

Clearly, resilience is a big deal to me; it's one of my core values and is central to everything I speak, coach, and write about. During adversity and transition, we discover traits we didn't even know we had—and they become part of our new DNA. The dictionary defines resilience as the power or ability to *return to the original form* or position after being *bent, compressed, or stretched*; elasticity. An ability to *recover from or adjust easily to misfortune or change.*

My life, regardless of my ability to be resilient, was not going to return to its original form; that ship had sailed. I was not going to be married to that man, live in that house, have that life ever again. The first definition is a curious one when you consider any living thing that is bent, compressed, or stretched—can it really return to its original form? The second definition seems more likely; the ability to recover and adjust to misfortune or change.

But, follow my train of thought for a minute...*original form*. Maybe that truly is the most beautiful definition of resilience. After all, one of the biggest lessons I learned was that I was not defined by my marriage—or lack thereof. I was more than someone's wife and mom, more than the job title I had, more than a street address. Those attributes contributed to who I was, but if those were stripped away, I wouldn't cease to exist.

"If I am what I have, and I lose what I have, then who am I?"
—Erich Fromm

The end of my marriage didn't signal the end of *me*, unless I decided that it did. In fact, that turbulent, questioning time was a catalyst to introspection, leading me to reconsider my priorities, my personal wants/needs/desires, my world view—and a myriad of possibilities. My *original form* was a woman who loved poetry and music, who could read and write voraciously, who enjoyed dancing and fun with friends. She liked deep discussions about important things and wasn't threatened if people disagreed—that was even better! As devastatingly painful as this experience was, I found myself returning to my original form and wondering how in the world I had deviated so far.

Let's think about the second definition: the ability to recover and adjust to misfortune and change. Well, that sounds just jolly, doesn't it? Just recover and adjust, by God. There are lots of "empowering" quotes and memes that make their way around women's circles. They are cute, and I have often used them myself. But seriously, they can be a little trite.

- She needed a hero, so that's what she became.

- Put on your big-girl panties and deal with it.

- Today I woke up with that whole princess warrior-save-the-world vibe.

- Think like a queen. A queen is not afraid to fail.

- Always feel pretty, no matter what you do.

I like these quotes when I am feeling powerful. When I do feel like a princess warrior. When I believe I am my own hero. But on those *other days*? Seriously, a queen is not afraid to fail? Who says? How many queens were interviewed to come to that conclusion? And always feel pretty no matter what? Come on, no pressure there! A friend of mine gave me a card that hangs on my bulletin board—it is so appropriate. It says, "I *am* wearing my big-girl panties, but they are starting to *bunch*!"

It's a short trip from self-empowerment to self-condemnation when we don't adapt as quickly as we think we should—or as quickly as conventional wisdom dictates. Our perspective can be skewed when we view everything that is going on around us—whether big or small—through the lens of current events. It seems like nothing is what it was when—in reality—much of life continues just the same. It's a huge gift to ourselves when we can step back and recognize that we are in the midst of a battle of sorts—and that we get tired. You aren't going to win every day. You aren't going to feel like a warrior princess every day. Some days will just be better than others.

Fatigue wars against effectiveness, so it's imperative for us to take care of ourselves. Consider thinking of yourself from the inside out and the outside in; in other words, emotional and social intelligence. You may have considered emotional intelligence (EQ) only in a workplace context, based on Daniel Goleman's landmark study. Goleman's theory focused on emotional intelligence as the main source of our capability and motivation, eventually affecting our professional success.

But from a personal standpoint, especially during times of change, emotional intelligence asks whether I am able to accurately recognize my own emotions, interpret them in the framework of what is going on in my life, and then manage or adjust as needed.

Let me give you an example. A few years ago I was working with a new corporate client. As I walked into the office for one of our first meetings, I received a distressing call from one of my sons—the kind of call you never want to receive from your kid. As I entered the conference room for our meeting, I had one of those brilliant moments of clarity that said, "You should postpone this meeting. You're not in a good place." That was one of those "voices in the head" I should have listened to! But, no, I pressed on. Tried to act as if nothing were wrong. And failed miserably. I ultimately ended the meeting in embarrassment: I looked unprepared and unprofessional. Had I simply said, "I'm sorry, I have a family emergency and need to reschedule," the client would have understood, and I would have maintained control of the situation.

But that takes a healthy dose of self-forgiveness. To be able to admit that I'm not Wonder Woman, my shields are completely down, and I owe it to myself to make the right adjustments. It also requires the fortitude to resist when people are pushing you to make decisions you might not be in the right frame of mind to make. Practicing good emotional intelligence during transition means managing myself from the inside out. How am I showing up? How do I need to adjust to maintain important relationships, and what decisions am I going to back-burner until a better time?

Developing social intelligence (SQ) is equally important. Am I accurately reading my interactions with others? How do I fit into certain social circumstances? It's more than the simplistic view of having "people skills," because social situations are a complex melding of experience, background, dynamics, and cultures. Anyone who has ever been invited to a cocktail party where they know no one can attest to this! In your new world order, circumstances may have changed that make some social constraints different, if not downright awkward. It's perfectly acceptable to say, "This just doesn't work for me anymore" and make adjustments.

Don't ignore the physical impacts of stress. I used to get so frustrated when I told my doctor I was experiencing <insert malady>, only to have it blamed on stress.

"My stomach is in knots all the time." *Oh, that's stress.*
"I have a tension headache every afternoon." *Oh, that's stress.*
"I think I'm having a heart attack." *Oh, that's stress.*
"My waistline has grown by three inches." *Oh, that's stress.*

OK. I get it. It's stress.
But surely there is something that can be done, right?
Yes, reduce your stress.
ARRRRGGGGHHHH!

So believe me, I can hear your eyes rolling as I tell you we have to pay attention to the impact stress has on our bodies. The side effects are scary—and they only increase our stress! I'm not going to list all the physical things we should do to minimize stress; you know them as well as I do. But ignore stress at your peril! Several times I thought I could just power through and ignore the warning signals my body was sending me. Once I ended up in the emergency room in the middle of the night with my back completely seized up in spasms. Only a massive, elephant-strength muscle relaxant provided relief.

Along with physical exercise, journaling, eating right, and all the other recommended stress-preventing lifestyle changes, I'd like to share one of my all-time favorites: The Serenity Prayer.

> God grant me the serenity to accept the things
> I cannot change,
> Courage to change the things I can,
> And wisdom to know the difference.

More than something recited at 12-step programs, I believe this is a beautiful mantra for life.

- **Accept the things I cannot change.** When it's three o'clock in the morning and you can't turn off the movie trailers in your head that are replaying every bad decision you've ever made…or when you're stuck in an endless loop of "if only's"…it can be incredibly comforting, freeing, and centering to accept that some things you simply cannot change.

- **Courage to change the things I can.** Introspection has opened your eyes to the changes you must make in your life, but they are hard. It requires letting go of the old and swinging out over that chasm that leads to the new. It takes courage.

- **And wisdom to know the difference.** There is nothing more heart-crushing than continuing to punish yourself for not being able to change something over which you had no control. This one might be the hardest one of all, especially for recovering control freaks like me. We really have such little control over anything except ourselves. Trust your own wisdom, and let it go.

I've also found the Serenity Prayer a great Resilience Factor Measurement tool. When new circumstances come up—as they inevitably do—rather than fall back into my old patterns of self-blame, I remember that I am resilient. I am not in charge of the world. I am only the boss of me.

Chapter 8

Defining A New Measurement

When I was no longer someone's wife, my yardstick for success needed adjustment. I was proud I had been married so long, lived in a nice neighborhood, and had a big house, three kids, one cat, and a mountain of debt. *"We"* was an oft-used pronoun: *We* went to church together, *we* had future plans, *we* liked certain shows, comedians, artists. *We* were a unit.

Practically overnight, *we* became *me,* and a lot of things didn't fit anymore. When I went to church it seemed everyone was married and part of an intact family. I had never noticed that before—and it wasn't true—but being part of a churchgoing family had been an integral part of my identity. And now it wasn't. *We* used to do home improvement projects together, but that was no longer possible. After all, there was no house to improve; I lived in a small, rented condo.

Things had changed. Whatever the dream was, it was over. What happens when we continue to hang on to a dead dream? It's hard to escape the victim cycle when we constantly look back at the "if only," when we continue to rehash the "woulda, coulda, shouldas" as if that could change anything in the present. If we're honest with ourselves, it wasn't all that perfect. If we're not careful, we can experience revisionist history in which we romanticize the thing that never was.

One of my kids started getting into trouble not long after my husband and I separated. He was cutting class, smoking, hanging out with undesirables—general mess-up stuff. I was exhausted, working overtime because we needed the money, racked with guilt because I wasn't home, and trying to balance it all. In my irrational mind, I thought, *if only my marriage hadn't broken up, he wouldn't be getting into so much trouble. None of this would be happening. We would still be the perfect, TV Land family.* Only we weren't. Another mother from my old neighborhood reminded me that our sons had been getting into the same kind of trouble before the divorce. Revisionist history.

There were many examples like this. My before and after lives were so different it was tempting to imagine how wonderful life would be if everything just went back to the way it was. The problem was, despite the turbulence and unpleasant circumstances, *I had changed.* I no longer identified with the woman whose value was defined by her marriage. I was discovering what I stood for, what mattered to me, the values I wanted to align with, new life priorities.

I had changed. The old measurement no longer fit. I needed a way to define success based on my experience and my new normal. Goals began to take on a new meaning. In business, goals are important. We have quarterly goals, strategic goals, project goals. It's equally important in life to set goals for ourselves: financial goals, retirement goals, and so forth. But the goal that came to mean the most to me was one I would never fully achieve; it was a goal I determined to chase for the rest of my life. It was The Resilience Factor. The Resilience Factor became my new measurement of success.

This new measurement says I am a full participant in the events of my life; I am not just on the receiving end. Things don't happen *to* me; they happen *with* me and *around* me. Once we determine not to let the events of our lives derail us, we have the ability to embrace change and write the next chapter. Goals are moving targets, my friends. Those personal goals we set for ourselves—what happens when we don't quite make them? When we miss the deadline, or only partially complete the task? We adjust; we erase the due date and put in another! Every step forward takes us that much further from where we were.

When circumstances shift—and they do—how do we measure the outcome's success? If we are able to fall back, regroup, and move forward with a Plan B, or C, or however many it takes while remaining steadfast to the things we say are the most important to us—that's success. Turnaround doesn't always happen immediately. Being resilient and faithful, even while waiting out the storm, are markers of success.

Redefining One's Life Options, or Teaching an Old Dog New Tricks

I began reading a great daily journal that has opened my eyes
to a lot of new thoughts
Reminded me of a lot of old, forgotten thoughts
And clarified a lot of jumbled, misguided thoughts.
I am discovering that there are so many souls like mine
Hungry for a deeper meaning to life, a simpler meaning,
One that really gets to the bones and marrow of our lives.

That in the rush to achieve, or succeed—or hell, just complete-
something-for-once—
We lose sight of what the goal was to begin with. Life itself.
It had been so long since I had enjoyed just living
Without it being an activity to produce a finished product.

I need uniformity, order, and goals in my life
And I have allowed that thirst for order to drive my every
movement and plan.

Then, all at once, my life had no order.
All the plans were canceled, all the deliverables recalled.
All the designs reengineered.

Hallelujah. I am forced to start again.
What matters to me? Does Pattie have a five-year plan?
Does Pattie want a five-year plan?
Can Pattie survive without a plan at all? (Well, to be real, I
don't think so.)

But how about goals with no dates attached? How about suggestions and maybes and
Bets wagered on my success?
How about if I make a friend of Life instead of my adversary?

It could happen…I could win. I could win some of them.
I could maybe even choose the ones I win and choose the ones I lose.
I like that…I like that very, very much.

—Pattie Vargas, 1995

Chapter 9

It's Always Good News/Bad News

Working on my Resilience Factor is an ongoing, never-ending project. After I remarried, I worked for an engineering company in the Bay area. It was a good job; I loved the company, I enjoyed the people I worked with. But the job itself was not particularly fulfilling or rewarding, and I was growing restless. I was introduced to the CEO of a small startup and, over the course of a few meetings, was convinced I had met the CEO of my dreams—the CEO I had always hoped existed but had not yet found. Ethics-driven, values-based, committed to the needs of the customer and the employee, and dealing transparently with the Board of Directors.

Imagine my excitement when the CEO of my dreams offered me the *job* of my dreams: the chance to build a corporate infrastructure from the ground up, based on the values we seemed to share. It was the chance of a lifetime, so I made the leap from relative security to a chance for something amazing.

You've probably guessed the outcome already. Despite rapid hiring and building expansion, the sales projections were all smoke and mirrors, and the ability to deliver on promises non-existent. Within six months I laid off more than 75 percent of the workforce, some of whom had been there less than a month. I was included in the final reduction in force.

It would be a gross understatement to say I felt shocked and angry; the feeling of betrayal was intensely personal because I had believed wholeheartedly in the integrity of the CEO and the rest of the leadership team (of which I had briefly been a member.) You might be thinking I should have known better (thank you, Accuser)—and maybe I should have. Nevertheless, there I was, suddenly and unexpectedly unemployed for the *first time in my life*.

In the days following, I did the usual: applied for unemployment for the first time ever (a demoralizing, frustrating, and dehumanizing procedure if ever there was one), contacted my network and recruiters, and started chasing down job leads. All of these were proactive and positive actions, and gave me some feeling of control over the situation. There were also the not-so-positive actions, like the happy hours, phone calls, and lunch meetings with some of the others who had been tossed out. That led to some fun leadership bashing, important shared intel—and a whole lot of negativity.

As time went by and the offers coming my way were both limited and uninteresting, I began to entertain a downward-spiral narrative: you're too old to get hired, no one will pay you what you're accustomed to, you should have never left the stable job, and so forth. Every lost opportunity or disappointment reinforced the story and, left unchecked, that narrative could have become my reality.

One day I met one of my former coworkers for lunch; it was a pleasant meal and mostly positive. As I walked away, I was struck by a moment of clarity—an *aha* moment that pretty much slapped me upside the head. I realized the parallel in this circumstance to the breakup of my marriage so many years before: unexpected, abrupt, and unfair. The similarity in the feelings of betrayal and inequity was enlightening—no, it was shocking. In the middle of the chaos of plans interrupted, I knew I had the opportunity to transition successfully through this mine field. It wasn't going to look quite like I had expected; it was going to be different. But it was up to me to write the next chapter.

When we step back from that victim precipice, we open ourselves to possibility. Sometimes they are possibilities we wouldn't have considered before, and they might not be all that attractive at the time. But we don't have to label a possibility as "good" or "bad." It is merely an option we can take—or not. When we aren't victims, we have choice. And that puts power right back where it should be—with us.

One of the possibilities I began to explore was to return to consulting full-time. Over the years I had maintained a coaching and speaking practice, but it was a "sidebar" to my day job. I continued to seek out full-time opportunities, but I also began to build out a practice. And one day, it was clear the "sidebar" was the direction I was meant to follow. Counsel from my Inner Circle helped me make that decision, as did the work that began to materialize. This was one of those options we could label "good," if we were going to assign a label. As you follow along here, my story can begin to resemble one of those "good news/ bad news" jokes, which hold a great deal of life truth!

Another possibility my husband, Tony, and I had to consider was how to reduce expenses and pay down debt. So we made the decision to sell our home and rent for a while. I'd categorize this option as "neutral." As much as I loved the house, my husband and I had long ago learned that "home is wherever we are together," and houses come and go. The chance to downsize and reduce expenses was far more attractive, and it felt wise and right to be proactive.

We loved the town we lived in, and it fit our lifestyle perfectly. But the rental market was tight and expensive, so we considered moving to Vacaville. At the time, the only thing appealing about this option was that my son, daughter-in-law, and granddaughter lived there, so it meant more face time with them. Decision made, we loaded up the U-Haul and headed for our new home.

Remember the continuum metaphor? Points on the continuum show the job loss, the sale of the house, and the move to Vacaville. Notice that some points on our continuum are a response to an unexpected event, while others are proactive and measured decisions. The thing to note is that I've learned to take control whenever and wherever I can, because so much in life is outside of our control.

As noted in Chapter 5, one aspect of control involves controlling the thoughts in my head and the conversations I engage in.

Instead of continuing the pity parties with some of my former coworkers, I connected with other impacted employees and offered my assistance to them. Sometimes it was just a pep talk; other times it was an introduction to a hiring manager or a letter of recommendation. I chose to be a light in their world and, by doing so, was in turn encouraged by my ability to provide value for them.

Around this time I reread John Maxwell's book *Sometimes You Win, Sometimes You Learn.* I decided to host a book study for anyone in my community who was interested in learning about and exercising their Resilience Factor. Talking to others about the power adversity has to bring about growth and maturity leads to self-reflection and, possibly, a sharp kick in the pants. I met some wonderful people in that book study and enjoyed some powerful, mind-altering discussions. It's in the doing that we are healed.

Fast forward a few months, and the move to Vacaville became much more than a circumstantial decision. My son and daughter-in-law became pregnant with twin girls. It was a happy and exciting time—until the girls made an emergency arrival eleven weeks early. In the midst of this frightening experience, we were so grateful we lived close by and could provide both tangible and emotional support when they needed it most.

To take any single tick point on my life continuum and make a judgment about any one of them would be short-sighted and poorly informed.

Chapter 10

Don't Be A Pinball In Someone Else's Machine

In the early days following my divorce, I had so much to do, so many decisions to make, it was exhausting. Sometimes, I found myself fighting the urge to settle for something less than I deserved. Some days it was a struggle just to get out of bed; I am so thankful I had three kids expecting me to be an adult.

Settling took a lot of shapes and forms, from trying to convince myself the mind-numbing, soul-crushing job I was doing was sustainable, to justifying the selfish behavior of a potential suitor because he had a good job and was looking to settle down. Yes, I actually considered that, and I can't believe it myself. But it all made some kind of crazy sense back in those days of upheaval. I had to decide the path to take—be the Master (or mistress, for those of you who mistrust gender-neutral pronouns) of My Universe or continue to be a pinball in someone else's machine. What would each of those choices look like?

To be the Master of My Universe would require intentional living, not just existing. Up to this point I had been moving from action item to action item, always putting out fires, missing the *now* while hoping for a better *future*. Taking charge would mean determining my own criteria for what I wanted and deserved in a friend, lover, or career, and then sticking to it.

To continue to be a pinball in someone else's machine (I love this metaphor) would mean I simply reacted every time the plunger fell and sent me careening from side to side, point A to point B, powerless to do anything more than survive the game. With each pull the game changes, so there is no accountability for the ball—it is just a victim.

I had a coaching client, Laura, who had experienced a great deal of upheaval all at once: her husband retired, they moved to a town where she knew no one, and the telecommuting privilege at the company where she worked was coming to an end. She had assumed the persona of the pinball, with an endless litany of confusion and loss of her compass. As she contemplated how terrible it would be to have to start commuting into the office each day, I asked if she had considered any alternatives.

I hoped she would get creative. Maybe she could look for another opportunity in the company that would still allow her to work from home, investigate a job change, consider other streams of income—anything. But she was in full-blown panic mode! The plunger had been pulled. She was going to go broke, she was going to be stuck at home (did I mention her husband had just retired?), and she would never be a valuable member of her community again.

I allowed the frantic stream to continue for three minutes. (For those who find yourselves on the receiving end of that kind of downward-spiraling rant, three minutes is the max allowable.) I then calmly asked her to do something for me; I asked her to complete an assignment before we met again. First, I asked her to document her personal and professional demise—how she was going to never work again, go broke, become housebound, and be friendless forever. I told her to be very specific, describe in great detail what that was going to look like, the kind of person she would become, how her husband would behave, the luxuries they would have to forfeit, what kind of food they would eat, which utilities they would cut off first. Initially, she was silent. Then she laughed nervously and said she didn't understand why I wanted her to do this.

I didn't let her off the hook. I scheduled my next check-in with her and ended the meeting.

A week later a different woman showed up. Laura had completed the assignment—I think she was afraid I would fire her if she didn't—but ended up so ashamed of her self-victimization, she decided that was *not* how the story was going to go. She hated the picture she was painting and, somewhere in the middle, it turned into an exploration of possibilities. It led to an open and heartfelt discussion with her husband about her fear of the future—hers and theirs. Long story short, they ended up opening a business in a field they both enjoyed, made new friends, and began a new journey.

That was the beginning of Laura's Resilience Experience, but I can assure you it's not one-and-done. She will find many opportunities along the way to exercise her Resilience Factor. But I know beyond a shadow of a doubt that this instance will be the one she looks back to—when she remembers she didn't die, but emerged a victor over her circumstance.

There's an acronym I love: WOWSE—With Or Without Someone Else. Not everyone will be excited about your decision to be Master of Your Universe instead of the Pinball in Someone Else's Game. Not everyone will approve or agree with the direction you are taking with your life. That's OK – you aren't looking for their approval. Decide you are going to stay the course WOWSE.

Chapter 11

God, Google
And Grace

Seriously…again? The digital number on my bedside clock reads "4:30," but I don't even have to look to know. I refer to it as the "witching hour," but a more accurate title would be the "worry hour." This phenomenon of waking at the "witching hour" began not long after my marriage ended and, honestly, there was much to worry about back then. But as the years went by, the insomnia became more and more pervasive, until sleeping through the night became a luxury.

Some interesting data about worry in general: I read that about 40 percent of the things we worry about are things that aren't likely to happen. Thirty percent of our worries concern things in the past that can't be changed. By my calculation, that means the majority of things that keep me up at night are a ridiculous waste of precious sleep. So what about the rest? Twelve percent are baseless worries about our health, and 10 percent are petty, miscellaneous worries. Keeping score? During the "worry hour," only 8 percent of what I'm ruminating over deals with legitimate issues.

As a Christian, I know that worry indicates a faith deficiency—yet another thing to worry about (I can do this all night if I'm not careful). If the statistics I cited above are accurate, worrying is a colossal waste of productivity—not to mention a suck of energy and joy. Intellectually I understand this; I coach others, as well as myself, to distinguish between the things we can change and the things we can't. Most of the time I'm relatively successful in managing the self-talk and personal condemnation, but I hit a roadblock not long ago that nearly did me in. I warned you earlier that the Resilience Factor isn't one-and-done and, during this stretch of time, I had to pull out all the stops to regain my equilibrium.

The challenge came when a series of personal blows within my family came one upon another, followed by some frightening health issues. Any of the circumstances on their own would have been painful, but as I dealt with one, here came another and then another on top of that until my strength was drained. In that emotionally weakened state, I came down with the mother of all flu viruses—and, to add insult to injury, it was Christmas. Yay. It's the most wonderful time of the year—unless you're sick in heart, mind, and body.

Sharing this story is difficult, but I do so to encourage others—to demonstrate that, no matter how many times we fall, we don't ever have to be down for the count. During this dark period, which lasted more than three months, I was convinced it was over for me.

That wasn't the first time in my life I had to battle my way back from the edge. As a very young woman, thoughts of suicide were ever-present; I considered the ways it could be done to inflict the least amount of pain on my family and have the least possible impact on the small world around me. The more I thought about it, the more rational an idea it became. I began to believe it was the antidote to heartache, pain, and loneliness. The notion of ending your own life is a seductive idea that gains momentum the longer you contemplate it, but the consequences are never presented in equal terms. After all, your mind is generating these thoughts, which lead to feelings of hopelessness. It's a vicious circle that, left unchecked, can lead to actions that can't be undone.

Fortunately for me, I rediscovered my faith at the lowest possible time in my life. At age 21, I began to believe that God loved me and had a plan for me, even when I couldn't see it and was pretty sure I had irreparably ruined my life by the choices I had made.

Fast forward many decades, and I found myself back in the darkness, overwhelmed by the challenges described above. I was worried about family members, frightened by health issues, wishing I could wake up and Christmas would be over! Each of the 8 percent legitimate worries had the power to bring past decisions and circumstances roaring back to the front of my mind. If my marriage hadn't ended, this would have never happened. If I hadn't taken that job, this other thing would have never happened. If I had paid more attention to finances, everything would be different. The "if/then" scenarios were never-ending, the abuse I heaped upon myself merciless. In my weakened physical and emotional state, suicide came calling again, with the seductive reasoning I thought I had overcome so many years before. The worry hour arrived earlier and earlier each night, as I found myself awake in the dark, struggling to gain a foothold on sanity.

Regardless of where we live, I always stake out a space in our home that is my reading and meditation spot. During this time, I had a comfy spot in a seldom-used room, with a view of the front yard and our tree-lined street. In the wee hours of the morning it was quiet and softly lit, and that's where I went to do battle. Because that's what it was, my friend. I was battling against the lies in my head that were telling me I was finished; that death would be preferable to the pain I was in. That, ultimately, everyone would be just fine— maybe not better without me, I'm too smart for that lie—but they would be just fine.

The tools in my arsenal included—in no particular order because I was grasping at straws—my Bible, my own past writings in my journals (meaning "physician, heal thyself"), other writers, music, and Google. Google? Yes, Google. Many, many nights I played Google roulette, where I simply typed a thought into the search engine to see what came up. Without fail, something of meaning turned up—something that provided a perspective I gravely needed. I found expository writings, apologetics, and inspirational stories and poems that replaced the voice in my head and helped me crawl away from the edge.

One night I came across the lyrics to a song I knew long ago. The song is "Worn[2]" by Tenth Avenue North. The lyrics perfectly describe a soul that feels crushed by the weight of the world and, without judgment, recognizes what it means to feel broken, weak and worn down.

Rather than instruct me to "just have faith," or "simply believe," the writers of this song knew the despair and sense of failure that dominate when we start at a negative position. Just the fact that someone had written such lyrics helped me understand I was part of a compassionate community, and gave me hope and strength.

Music has always been a healing medium for me; I've found it easier to replace destructive thoughts with powerful lyrics when I find myself struggling. During this dark period, lyrics that came to mind often led me to research topics that further enhanced my healing. Carole King's "Tapestry" led me to consult The Google on thoughts about tapestries.

I learned that while the front of the tapestry is beautiful, the back of it is chaotic. There are pieces of thread, called "weft" threads, just dangling as if forgotten. But the placement is actually quite intentional.

I began to consider each circumstance in my life at that time as a discreet, individual part of the overall picture (or tapestry) of my life. In my state of mind, I only saw a huge mass of twisted threads, knots, and chaos when, in reality, the other side was exquisitely beautiful. You can't have the good without the bad—without suffering and adversity, we would be foolish, self-centered people, useless to anyone around us. The overall combination of experiences keeps the "weft threads" from overwhelming us.

What are the lessons I learned that came from this despair-ridden time?

1. Don't think I'm immune; I'm not. Just because I know the value and importance of having a resilient heart and mind doesn't mean the waves can't knock me down.

2. The quicker I get up, the better off I'll be. Despite the weight of sorrow, find a way back. Call a friend, talk to your spiritual advisor, read, pray, sing…but don't isolate. Hope is killed in isolation. When I finally shared with someone how frail and fragile I felt, they were able to come alongside and offer support.

3. Self-care is as critical to my well-being as breathing. Even before the disappointments arrived I had slacked off on my exercise, meditation time, and healthy eating. I was so busy being busy I had no time for me—leaving me vulnerable and exposed.

Our lives tend to fall into a before and after—before we experienced our wake-up call, and the lessons and experiences that came after. And even though I wish it didn't take some kind of event to bring us back to life, I am grateful that they happen. But now what? Unless we want our life to be one abrupt about-face after another, it's a good idea to learn how to stay the course. Lessons aren't worth much if we don't remember what we learned—that's like the curse in the movie *Groundhog Day*. What torture to wake up in the aftermath of some happening and scream, "Oh, no, not again! I thought I *learned* this lesson!"

If we think of our life as a continuum, we can look back and see a progression of actions, occasions, and episodes from our past and assume there are more to come. The continuum analogy falls down a bit in that we don't have a prescribed point in time when the story will end. Nevertheless, we can characterize the points on the line—past, present and future—as a collection or sequence of experiences that make up our story.

There is great comfort, at least for me, in the continuum metaphor. It reminds me not to judge my success as a human being based on any one point in time. Separated from the full story, I can make hurtful and even dangerous judgments about a situation. But put in the context of the greater whole, I gain perspective.

Chapter 12

The More I Learn, The Less I Know

There's an interesting concept in social psychology called Fundamental Attribution Error that manifests itself in a variety of ways. Basically, it means that when we do well—we're successful in our careers, our children are high achievers, we enjoy happy marriages, we make lots of money—it's because we deserved it. We worked harder, behaved better, did all the right things, and are worthy of all our success. Conversely, when things are not going well for us, it's someone else's fault. The game was rigged, the environment was unfair, there was simply no way to beat the odds. The error comes when we turn that lens on others; if they are struggling in their careers, their children are in trouble, their marriages end in divorce—well, *they* screwed up. Their situation must be due to a character flaw somewhere.

Psychologist Paul Piff, along with a team of Berkley researchers, conducted a study to determine the correlation of perceived privilege with behavior. In the experiment, students played rigged games of Monopoly. One student, selected by a random roll of the die, started the game with more money, was able to roll two dice instead of one, and collected the typical $200 each time he passed Go. The other student—whose game piece was an *elf shoe* compared to the other player's *race car*—could only roll one die, and only collected $100 each time he passed Go.

Neither player's actions had any bearing on how the odds were stacked. The wealthier player hadn't earned that money; the poorer player had not wasted any money. *Nothing either of them had done caused them to have more or less privilege.* But as the games progressed, the wealthier players became more aggressive and more boastful, verbally expressing how much better they were than the other player. Their physical actions became more aggressive: they raised their arms in victory and engaged in other overt displays of winning. Despite the fact they were not responsible in any way for their success, they displayed a sense of entitlement—their success reduced their ability to feel empathy for the other player.

That was an experiment in a controlled environment. But there is a parallel in society when we consider the Fundamental Attribution Error—it seems to be in our makeup to need an explanation for everything that happens. The winning Monopoly player was a better, more clever player. The loser was lazy and slow. But sometimes there is no explanation—and the answers that others supply *severed from experience* are not helpful. Experience is what separates head knowledge from heart knowledge; experience locks in what I *know*. Here is the treasure, my friends. Overcoming obstacles, making the transition from then to now, brings about grace for others and hope for better days that can be dignifying and life-changing!

I believe—I *know*—that adversity makes us better people. It needn't be a catastrophic, near-death, end-of-the-world kind of adversity, so don't worry if your challenges have been relatively minor. But advice from someone who has never experienced a single setback is empty—it's just theory. The power comes from the experience; no one can argue with what we have gone through.

Bill Gates said, "Success is a lousy teacher. It makes smart people think they can't lose." That is a profound quote. Without failure, we can't appreciate success—it came so easy we attribute it to our brilliance. Success can also lull us into thinking there is nothing we need to learn. Maybe I wouldn't have learned what I have learned if the story had gone a different way; for sure I wouldn't be the woman I am today.

Adversity is humbling. When we put together the strategic plan for our life, we don't include milestones of suffering: *here's where I lose my job, around here is where my house burns down*. But without hardship, our humanity is lacking. There's no depth to the relationships we have with others. I was so smart when I was younger, so smug. So sure that none of the negative events that have occurred in my life would ever happen. Adversity makes us better people; multidimensional, with more texture and a greater capacity to care for others.

We don't have to have exactly the same experience to become a partner in others' suffering, but there is great comfort and camaraderie as we come alongside, listen, and encourage. Our history can bring assurance: the confidence that we survived setbacks, and so will they. How incredibly freeing it is not to feel compelled to give an answer or solution—but simply to be there.

In a nutshell—the more I learn, the less I know. The more life I experience, the less qualified I feel to prescribe solutions for anyone. What I gain, though, is empathy. I'm less likely to attribute your failings to your character flaws and my successes to my awesomeness. In fact, I'm less likely to pass judgment on your situation at all. That lens could so easily swing back around to me.

That's the wisdom in developing your Resilience Factor. Because—face it—that Big Wake-Up Call isn't the last time you'll need to rely on it. It's never one-and-done. If you were hoping the end of this book was a series of encouragements from my now-perfect life, sorry to disappoint you. That's someone else's book—and frankly, I hate those books. They make me feel more inadequate than ever. Here's the reality: I struggle to stay the course on a daily basis. The Voice in The Head never stops; the lies that assault me from the media, describing the perfect life, relationship, body, and professional success, find their home inside my thoughts and—well, I've learned what can happen when I allow those thoughts to run wild and free!

There is no shortage of opportunity to apply what I've learned, and I should celebrate my progress. Every time I recognize the trap and adjust my thinking and behavior, it counts as a victory and signifies growth. Growth is important—without it, there is no life, only stagnation.

My Life
My life is my life.
It may not be the life I imagined
   The life I dreamed of
     The life I would proudly show off to others
Nevertheless, it's mine.

To denounce it would be to denounce
everything and everyone
that have made me what I am today.
And that would be cruel,
short-sighted
and foolish.

I have my bruises and scars to thank for my world view
Far more than the blessings I currently enjoy.
Blessings are nice—they are respites in the middle of life—
they are not earned or deserved.

But if you love me, if *I* love me,
It's because of the darkness that led me—and continues to
lead me—
To the light.

        —Pattie Vargas, 2017

Acknowledgments

Even though I am a frequent and prolific writer, this book was a hard one to write. I was torn between the need to tell my story to reassure others they can recover from the unexpected blows of life, and the fear I would sound like I hadn't moved on at all. This story is very personal and, like most stories, affects and includes others. In the end, the desire to serve outweighed the fear of exposure and, with the encouragement of so many Champions in my Inner Circle, here it is.

First of all, thanks to Bethany Kelly and Michelle Bergquist of Women Lead Publishing. Bethany's guidance and gentle prodding kept me on task when I got bogged down and discouraged. Michelle's unwavering belief that I could do it made me afraid to fail!

The women who have gone before me and blazed a trail with their experiences, failures, and successes have paid it forward over and over again. Whether through books, music, poetry, or conversation, their contribution to the growth in my life can never be repaid. In deep gratitude, I pay it forward, as well.

Much of what I know about resilience, responsibility, and unconditional love was imparted by my mom and dad and modeled by my brother and sister. I don't dare be less than that.

And, of course, thanks, God. Your love never fails. Your purpose for my life is worked out in the storms and dreams of everyday living, working with me as I am, not as I should be. That's a grace I'll never fully comprehend.

Resources/For More Information

I am passionate about helping others discover, increase, and exercise their Resilience Factor. I am available to speak at conferences and workshops, as well as provide one-on-one coaching. If you've never written a personal Mission Statement, request my simple, step-by-step template and proclaim your purpose for living. Every step forward is a step away from where you've been!

You can register on my website at www.thevargasgroup.net to receive my blog posts, information on upcoming events, and other news. You can also follow me:

Facebook at https://www.facebook.com/TheVargasGroup-Coaching/

Twitter: @pattiev

LinkedIn: https://www.linkedin.com/in/pattievargas/

Let's continue to support one another on our Resilience Journey. I look forward to connecting with you!

Notes

1. Edwina Trentham teaches English at Asnuntuck Community College in Enfield, Connecticut, and also teaches courses in women's poetry in the graduate liberal studies program at Wesleyan University. Her poems have appeared in a number of periodicals and anthologies, including *At Our Core: Women Writing About Power.*

2. Tenth Avenue North is an American contemporary Christian music band from West Palm Beach, Florida, that takes its name from an east-west road in Palm Beach County. The song "Worn" first appeared on the studio album Struggle in 2012.

About the Author

Pattie Vargas is a recognized leader in behavioral, organizational, and personal change. She coaches individuals and teams through the twists and turns of change, helping them gain personal perspective, encouragement, and self-management by strengthening their personal *Resilience Factor*. Whether it's organizational change, professional change, or a life change—it all affects us *personally*. Flexibility and adaptability are the key ingredients in increasing your ability to overcome and *thrive*.

Pattie speaks frequently at conferences on the topics of change management, personal resilience, team dynamics, and issues facing women in the workplace. Her delivery is humorous, practical, and backed by years of personal experience, both painful and pleasant!

Pattie holds a master's degree in organizational management and a bachelor's degree in business management. She is certified in the use of DiSC behavioral assessments and is a certified speaker, coach, and trainer with The John Maxwell Company.

Happy to call Northern California home, Pattie enjoys the wine country, sampling new varietals, and exploring foodie hangouts with her husband, Tony. They have one extremely large cat named Rocco and love spending time with their granddaughters, Halle, and twins Adalynne and Laynie.

women lead
P U B L I S H I N G™

Women Lead Publishing is dedicated to serving women authors. Let us support you and translate your expertise, passion, thoughts, and wisdom into a published book.

If you've always dreamed of writing a book and becoming a published author, contact us to schedule a book discovery session for your next big book concept and big idea!

www.womenleadpublishing.com

800-591-1673

Made in the USA
San Bernardino, CA
28 April 2018